Can you see me?

Elder Stephanie Coleman-Oliver

Copyright © October 2017 Elder Stephanie Coleman-Oliver

All rights reserved. No part of this book may be reproduced in any form or by any means without prior consent of the author, except in brief quotes used in reviews.

Scriptures taken from the Holy Bible, King James Version

Pureheart Publishing Inc.
Thomasville, NC 27360
www.pureheartpublishinginc.com

ISBN-13: 978-1547109098

ISBN-10: 1547109092

Can You See Me?

My prayer for you is: *Father within this day we ask that you open up our minds and hearts to receive what you are about to release to us. We thank you for giving us the necessary tools that will guide us through our life. So Father give us physical, mentally, and emotional strength, be our guide throughout this book that we may have a better understanding about ourselves. I pray that all find strength, comfort, and hope on every page you read and the power to release. I pray that all that read this book will have a LIFE CHANGING EXPERIENCE with God. Amen*

Dedication

This book was birthed from my pain, sorrows and struggles, but God has given me the insight by way of vision to express myself to all. I encourage you my brethren to rise above where you are and began to walk in your God's given purpose. So I dedicate this book to all men and women who have been broken down by the trials of their situations or circumstances.

Acknowledgments

Thank you does not measure my gratitude to the following people:

Life Changing Experience Outreach Worship Center *for always pushing, believing in and loving me throughout the years.*

Bishop Steven W Clay *for shaping and molding me*

Bishop Dr. George Jackson *for guiding, instructing and enriching me through education to reach beyond my potential*

Apostle James H. Carter *for giving me guidance in pulpit leadership*

Dr. Herbert Miller *for his instruction and exemplifying how to be an effective leader*

Dr. Carrie Dudley *for the emptying of herself and pouring into me throughout my journey and standing on the wall just for me*

Apostle Marcia Rhoe *for opening up avenues for me to walk in and an educator in theological seminary school*

Walker Jackson of Chester, SC *for the encouragement and extra push of seeing my God giving writing ability through social media*

Pastor Linwood Thompson *for constantly speaking into me,* ***Deacon Carlos Thompson and church family of LTCC of Greensboro, NC*** *for supporting my endeavors.*

Ivey Louise Gaymon*, my loving Mother and prayer warrior who supports and constantly prays for me; making herself transparent before me*

*My loving Father **Calvin Henderson** for all his support*

My loving children, ***Larissa, Calvin, Elijah & Jaylan Makupson*** *thank you for being my inspiration and supporting me*

My Husband, ***Gayland Oliver*** *for supporting my calling and journey to be an effective leader for the Kingdom of God*

Elijah Makupson *for the sacrifice of time and helping me to cultivate what God has instructed me to do; to have so much patience and seeing the manifestation come forward even when we were faced with daily adversities*

Motoya Ward *for your time and support in helping me in meeting deadlines and producing excellent results*

Yolanda "Yogi" Turner *for her support and always enhancing the beauty that is within me for over twenty years*

Kendra Diggs *for expressing her God given gift through makeup artistry; Instagram/Facebook: Kendra Mua*

Deatrice Littles *for the many years of friendship and sisterhood*

David Porter *for the graphic design & many years of friendship*

*And from the heart of me, my loving **family, friends and social media family** who have walked with me through my journey, seen me grow and overcome life's challenges.*

TABLE OF CONTENTS

Foreword………………………………….…..	X
Introduction…………………………………..	1
Chapter 1 - I Got Lost……………………...	4
Chapter 2 - Finding Yourself……………..	9
Chapter 3 - Facing the Facts……………...	12
Chapter 4 - Commitment…………………..	14
Chapter 5 - Unwrap Your Heart…………..	17
Chapter 6 – Damaged But Not Destroyed………	20
Chapter 7 – Motivation Time……...………	25
Chapter 8 – Marriage, Forgiveness and Singleness…………………………..	29
Chapter 9 – Praise Got Me Out…………...	35
Chapter 10 – My Battle is No Longer a Secret…	41
Chapter 11 – Transformation Begins…………..	44
Chapter 12 – Stretch For It………………..	50
Chapter 13 – On the Wrong Road at the Wrong Time………………………………..	53
Chapter 14 – I Found a Way Out………...	57
Chapter 15 – Write It All Down…………..	60
Chapter 16 – Dare To Believe……………..	67
Chapter 17 – Leave It Up to Him…………	71
Chapter 18 – There Is a Place For You…………	74
Chapter 19 – At the Point of No Return………..	79
Chapter 20 – God's Promise To You………….	83
Chapter 21 – Rebound To Build……………..	88
Chapter 22 – I'm Not Running Back To You….	93
Chapter 23 – Purpose To Succeed……………..	97
Scripture References………………………..	100

FOREWORD

From the humble beginning of this journey with my Dear sister in Christ, we laughed, cried and grew together while allowing God to work in and through us. As individuals we are all faced with the trials of life; there may be times when you can't seem to see your way through. I pray you gain visibility through the fog as this book serve as a guiding light as a lighthouse to a broken vessel. Allow the healing to take place for peace to resonate in your heart, for without peace you're truly not free.

This book was created for you to interact and engage with self, a tool to study who you really are and who you are destined to become. So I say unto you let go, release and shake off all the things that doesn't serve you well or make you grow. Always count on God for He has a purpose and reason for all that we go through—pain, struggles, heartaches and disappointments, know that your faithfulness will be rewarded. Never give up!

~ Elijah Makupson

Introduction

I have been amazed how people go around and think that you have it all together, but yet they don't understand what you're carrying around in the inside. People go to church Sunday after Sunday wearing the same mask. A face of lies and listening to the sermon being preached and thinking to themselves is it hope for me? I know all about that very well because I too wore a face of flint; carrying myself with integrity, upright, and a smile but yet I was bleeding on the inside from the pain, holding it all together so those so close couldn't see. Sometimes, you have to go outside your element into a new environment and seek freedom and wholeness.

The Bible says "seek ye first the kingdom of God and all these things will be added unto you." You see, it's very important that we identify with our past setbacks to we can move forward with God and our inner peace. After you lay aside every weight of pain, fear, anger, even tears allow God to breathe new life into you by going on a sabbatical and spiritual fast. Fast every day for the things that have set you backwards, set goals for yourself daily and start by doing a self- evaluation. Think things through prayer. My motto is "for every problem there is a solution, but first you have to be real with yourself regarding the situation, circumstance, dilemma, or crisis. An alternate route is to take an index card each day, write a scripture on it and carry along with you throughout the day. You'll discover the more word you put into you the more it will help you build a relationship with God. Follow God and he will direct your path.

For a long time I often wondered in the back of my mind is there a place of happiness for me. Then one day as I was lying in bed I felt God's presence fall upon me and a still voice said, "I am your healer, you are restored". To me it was like a gift at Christmas and not knowing what was in the box with your heart racing with anticipation and excitement while tearing into the box to discover what the contents were. That's how God was, he was tearing into my soul, filling me with joy and peace, helping me to realize **my worth and value**. You may have been damaged but you have not been destroyed. You may have been broken into pieces, but God is about to bring you back to life. Say "God bring me back to life, revive me!" As you shout those words, I'm reminded of David in *Psalms 40:1* when he said I waited patiently for the Lord and He inclined into me and heard my cry. I'm so glad to know that when we call on our Lord and Savior Jesus Christ He will hear us and meet our every need. Let's go on a journey; within this book I ask that you follow the steps to recovery.

Follow the map: Trusting God completely means having faith to know that God knows what's best for your life and understand that with every road block a detour is built. And with every ending, is a new beginning. Remember it's a process.

Follow the map: When life's trials overcome you, and you have nowhere to turn. When you reached the very bottom, there are lessons you must learn. Rock bottom is good but remember a dead end street is just a place to turn around. God is working it out for you.
………...Lets begin

Chapter 1
I Got Lost

Many of us have suffered too many spiritual miscarriages and if we are not careful we will have a spiritual hysterectomy. We have to understand that timing is critical and also understanding the birthing process of God when He is trying to birth your purpose. What will happen if we aren't careful is that we will die without ever giving birth. You need to ask God to redirect your life and get up from the cemetery of your struggles. Things in life are time sensitive and when God has something for you to do, He can take it and give it to someone else you will or you will not abort what God is trying to do.

The biggest question is, what degree of value does one bring to your life? Recognize that there are some things that are in our lives that's dead, in fact a hindrance. We must realize that we are living in the cemetery of our troubles and going nowhere. And now it is time to revive what remains in us. Revive means to bring back to life or consciousness, aren't you glad you don't look like what you've been through.

Follow the map: If you stumble get back up and what happened yesterday no longer matters. Today's another day so get back on track and move closer to God, your dreams, and your goals. You can do it. Don't stop when you are tired, stop when you are done!! PUSH FORWARD!

I Got Lost

List some areas that affected you and put you in a lost state of mind.

_____   _____

_____   _____

_____   _____

_____   _____

_____   _____

Remember impure thoughts seek and decay the mind……release and let it go!

FOLLOW THE MAP: *When God pushes you to the edge of difficulty trust Him fully. There are two things that can happen he will either catch you when you fall or teach you how to fly. It's only a process.*

COME FACE TO FACE WITH YOURSELF: *Whenever you find yourself doubting how far you can go, just remember how far you have come. Remember everything that you have faced; all the battles you have won, and all the fears you have overcome. One who gains strength by overcoming obstacles possesses the only strength that can overcome adversity. And the struggle that you are in today is developing your strength for tomorrow.*

Journal your thoughts from this chapter:

Chapter 2
Finding Yourself

God first forgive me for harboring resentment against_____. Help me to overcome what happened and how it made me feel. Forgive me for treating others unkind as a result of my pain and help me to overcome how I treat myself from this day forward. I realize that prayer provides us with a key insight into how we can experience joy and an abundant life that Jesus told us we can have. "Give us this day our daily bread, and forgive us our trespasses as forgive those who trespass against and led us not into temptation but deliver us from evil for thy is the kingdom the power and glory forever amen."

Often times we have experienced a great amount of pain and we walk around numb it is very important that we identify with our past setbacks so that we can move forward with God and lay aside every weight of pain, fear, and anger and allow God to breathe new life into us. Set goals for yourself each day. Let's do an exercise each day using this decree:

I declare and decree whenever I find myself doubting how far I can go; I will remember how far I have come.

I declare and decree that everything that I have faced, all my battles, I have already won and all my fears I have already overcome. I realize one who gains strength by overcoming obstacles possesses the only strength that can overcome adversity. Friends understand the struggles that you are facing today are developing your strength for tomorrow. I DECLARE THAT YOU AND I ARE FEARFULLY AND WONDERFULLY MADE BY GOD.

Journal your thoughts from this chapter:

Chapter 3
Facing the Facts

LET'S FACE IT*: If you don't make the time to work on creating the life you want, you're eventually going to be forced to spend a lot of time dealing with a life you don't want. Some of us have had some setbacks and disappointment from other but I want you to say this on today: My setbacks may have amused you, but my comebacks are going to confuse you!*

Let's reposition our life by creating and listing the kind of life you want; write the vision make it plain.

_____

_____

_____

_____

REPOSITION TIME*: People say I'm making progress; but progress is impossible without change and those who cannot change their mindset cannot change nothing at all. What are you trying to change? First change your mindset! #forHeknowstheplansHehasforme*

Journal your thoughts from this chapter:

Chapter 4

Commitment

Are you committed? Without commitment nothing can happen. In this chapter, we will gain strength and character. Our first step is to examine our level of commitment. Leah has been giving to Jacob as a price but Jacob entered into a seven year commitment with her father because in the Biblical days you had to work for your bride. However Jacob was tricked, Leah was tendered eyed, meaning she was crossed eyed, not attractive or had no sexual appeal to her but her sister Rachael was beautiful. Leah was so hated by her sister Rachael that God open up her womb. It's amazing how people can deny you the oxygen of love. Once Jacob discovered he had been tricked and was given Leah to bride instead of Rachael to whom he preferred. Leah tried everything to try to win Jacob's love. Leah began to have children; the first to be born was named Simeon which means "maybe Jacob will see me". The second child was named Ruben in which I heard it means "that maybe if I give him this child then he would care". Levi the third child, Leah felt as if this child will join them together and he would be committed to her. The fourth child named Judah which means "Praise the Lord". Finally Leah came to a place where she said she was done trying to get this man that she was committed to for life to see her.

    Understand you cannot become a believer until you see your old life and change it. I believe Leah finally got it! She recognized that she was fighting a battle that was not hers. As a believer you have to realize that your old self is undone and that your vision is tangled and time is wasting until you see it, until you recognize your misery. So break barriers in your life and rise above where you are.

Journal your thoughts from this chapter:

Chapter 5
Unwrap Your Heart

If you see a person's soul and you discover that it may have a CRACK in it, gently pour LOVE into it and wait on the outcome. When it concerns the matters of your heart, your mistakes don't define your character, it's what you do after you make the mistakes that make all the difference. Remember your value doesn't decrease based on someone's inability to see your worth, love will still find you! Even if you're consumed with so much pain, praise your way through!

Although, if someone see that you are hurting and they don't do anything about it they don't love you and they definitely don't care about you; realize that no matter what you go through, with God, you can move any mountain, endure any struggle and be healed. It is beautiful when accept and experience God's love. Once you accept and experience God's agape love, He watches you take down your wall you've built around your heart and allow Him to come inside.

List six passages or verses from the Bible on love, copy on an index card and recite each day.

_____   _____

_____   _____

_____   _____

Journal your thoughts from this chapter:

Chapter 6
Damaged But not Destroyed After This

Where you are today is no accident GOD is using your situation you are in right now to shape you and prepare you for the place he wants to bring you to. GOD is turning your ashes into beauty.... so praise GOD for yesterday that took you through hell. GOD is going to bless you simply because of what you have endured. The Bible says Corinthians II 4:7-9 (NIV) 7 but we have this treasure in jars of clay to show that this all surpassing power is from God and not from us. 8 We are hard pressed on every side, but not crushed: perplexed, but not in despair: 9 persecuted, but not abandoned; struck down, but not destroyed.

These particular verses deals with the letters of the Apostle Paul to the Church at Corinth and are the most popular. The first letter deals with the behavior and correction in the church. While the second letter deals with Paul and how he gives us his autobiographical life story. It is in this chapter that he gives up details of his life, how he deals with issues that we currently have in the church. Paul deals with his personal attacks as it relates to his integrity and validity of being an apostle. The first century church was refusing to validate who he was because they felt like he had no true evidence, even though he had a Damascus road encounter that wasn't enough. Most of the time when God speaks to us you have to realize that no one has to hear you but God. So Paul tells us who he is and who he was as a minister. In chapter 2 Paul reference how ministry cannot be done in your own ability. He teaches us about the frailty of humanity. He displays to us how we need to be transformed and speaks to us in the chapter describing how it's like going from glory to glory. He also says, that it's a progression filled with difficulty. I could not

Understand how Paul got glory out of what he went through, but I realized it was glory because of how he managed all that he had gone through and saw glory in it. When we acknowledge the power of God, we can come out of anything; don't allow people to evaluate you while you are going through advise them to evaluate you as you're coming out.

Sometimes you have to turn the page to realize that there is more to your book of life then the page you are stuck on. Stop being afraid to move on and close this chapter of hurt, and never re-read it again. It's time for you to get what you deserve in life, and move on from the things that you don't deserve. Don't spend your days trying to correct your past, instead, let go and let God create something better for your future.

"When I let go of what I am, I become what I might be. When I let go of what I have, I receive what I need."

Now list six things you need to let go of that has damaged you:

_____   _____

_____   _____

_____   _____

"If you saw the size of the blessing coming, you would understand the magnitude of the battle you are fighting.

Food for thought: *What you need to do is attract what you expect, reflect what you desire, become what you respect, and mirror what you admire.* So don't wait for the world to recognize your greatness, but live it and let the world catch up to you.

Whenever you pursue greatness it makes people uncomfortable so be prepared to lose some people on your journey. So look at yourself in the mirror and say to yourself, I love me, and nothing will destroy me, and I'm not going to fall because God is carrying me and I am glad I don't look like what I've been through.

Journal your thoughts from this chapter:

Chapter 7

Motivation Time

The past is your lesson, the present is your gift and the future is your motivation. Let go of the things that can no longer be fixed. One of the things that I have learned is if you try to force a situation to come back together it will only get worst. God wants us to look beyond where we are in our lives and create a better environment. God will take the pain in your life and teach you how to trust Him. I love the Jabaz prayer because it helps you to be more intimate with God.

I Chronicles 4:10 "*Jabez called upon the God of Israel, saying, "Oh that you would bless me and enlarge my border, and that your hand might be with me, and that you would keep me from harm so that it might not bring me pain!"* And God granted what he asked." What's amazing is that Jabez past problems had pre-deposed him to the limitless possibilities of prayer, in other words when your mother name you pain that means his mother had to be in a bad place and your childhood had to be a trip. But somewhere in the middle of all the mess he knew how to call on Jesus.

The reason why some people don't understand why you go after God the way you do is because they don't know what you have come out of. It's what we go through that teaches us how to be a better person. It is through our pain that God teaches us how to trust Him. So getting back to Jabez, he sent out a request to God saying to Him "Bless me indeed", what's amazing to me is that he used the word "indeed". It was not a normal blessing, but he wanted an indeed blessing. We should say to ourselves God bless me indeed—enlarge my borders, increase my influence, don't restrict me and I don't want to be boxed in, but bless me indeed! When we pray God starts removing stones we need to say, God I deserve more than this, please give me a Jabez prayer and enlarge my territory because the space that I'm in isn't large enough.

What stones do you desire for God to remove and list six areas that you want God to enlarge?

God remove these stones:

_____   _____

_____   _____

_____   _____

God enlarge these areas in my life:

_____   _____

_____   _____

_____   _____

Journal your thoughts from this chapter:

Chapter 8

Marriage, Forgiveness and Singleness

What are some adversities that people struggle with? Forgiveness, marriage and all other things that set you back from the blessings of God. "Forgiveness" brings you out of your morning state.

In a marriage there are three things in life that leave and never return: WORDS, TIME, and OPPORTUNITIES. I'd rather live life accepting who I am and loving it, knowing I'm not perfect, then live my whole life pretending to be... in your marriage be careful who you pretend to be. you might forget who you really are...just be you!

In a marriage you must learn a new way to think before you can master a new way to be. However, In order to move forward in your marriage you have to know which direction you both are going. What DIRECTION are you going?

What direction would you like your marriage to go? List six ways in which you would like your marriage to go.

_____   _____

_____   _____

_____   _____

A quick reference guide to help build your marriage: Ecclesiastes 4:12, Ecclesiastes 9:9, Ephesians 4:2-3, Genesis 1:27-28, Hebrew 13:4, Mark 10:9, I Peter 4:8.

In the art of forgiveness sometimes you have to take a step back and realize what's important in your life. What you can live with, but most importantly what you can't live without. Don't let something that's long gone continue to control you. The only person that you are destined to become is the person you are destined to be.

Life asked death "Why do people love me but hate you?" death responded," Because you are a beautiful lie and I am the painful truth. It never stops hurting does it? Giving someone the best of you and watching them choose to do something else. Always remember everything in life is a reflection of the choice you have made.

Reflection time: Write and mail a letter to those you need to forgive.

_____
_____
_____
_____
_____
_____
_____
_____
_____
_____

Signed,
I've let it go!

Embrace your singleness; it's a gift from God. The hardest thing isn't losing him or her; it's forgiving yourself for falling in love with them. If life and its trials overcome you with nowhere to turn and when you reached the very bottom there will be lessons you must learn. However, sometimes rock bottom is good but remember a dead end street is just a place to turn around.

If you stumble, never quit get back up. What happened yesterday no longer matters. Today is another day so get back on track and move closer to God, rediscovering your dreams and goals. You can do it and don't stop when you are tired. Stop when you are done! #PUSHFORWARD

Know who you are, you are one of strength, courage and dignity; one who values yourself and fight for what you believe in. Do not give up on your dreams regardless of how many obstacles that stands in your way. After you have been broken you can stand through anything. I am fearfully and wonderfully made by God. Embrace your singleness!

How do you embrace your singleness? List four areas that you embrace.

_____   _____

_____   _____

Embracing your singleness God's way:
I Corinthians 7:7, I Corinthians 7:28,
I Corinthians 7:32-34, Matthew 19:11

Journal your thoughts from this chapter:

Chapter 9

Praise Got Me Out

Acts 16:25-26 ^{25} But about midnight Paul and Silas were praying and singing hymns of praise to God, and the prisoners were listening to them; ^{26} and suddenly there came a great earthquake, so that the foundations of the prison house were shaken; and immediately all the doors were opened and everyone's chains were unfastened. If you are not too shy repeat after me, say "Praise Got Me Out!" I wanted to start by telling you how God lead me to this text and how he lead me to this chapter. I was asking God to lead me to biblical text that would reflect on how good God is and how good he would stick with you even in bad times. So God lead me to the tent maker from Tarsus alone with Silas who was both in the joint and I wanted to show you how even they praised God in the mist of their difficult and arduous situation. This is a time of thank you; this is a time of being grateful. To me no biblical text can reflect on how to praise God in the worst of situation like this particular text in Acts 16.

In Acts, chapter 16 Paul said "that we were going to Asia but the Holy Spirit said no." "We were going to preach but the holy spirit said no, even though we had good intentions but the holy spirit said "don't go that way", that got me tripping because sometimes you can mean well and God will still say no. What do you do when you meant to go in one direction and the Holy Spirit block you. We wanted to go to Asia but the Holy Spirit forbid us and said no you have to go this way. All of us know that there was this little girl that had this spirit in her that needed to be cast out by Paul plus there was some other prisoners that needed to hear some praise. Can I advise you that God would manipulate certain situations so that he would get you where he wants you to be.

God works in mysterious ways, aren't you glad that God shuts some doors in your life in order to open up some others ones? It was God that allowed that man or woman break up with you so that he can open up a new door. God knows how to shut a door so that he can open up a new door for your life.

List seven doors that you would like God to shut in your life so you can move:

DOORS

1. _____
2. _____
3. _____
4. _____
5. _____
6. _____
7. _____

Dear God, thank you for shutting the door!

Dear You, make peace with the mirror and watch your reflection change. The secret of change is to focus all of your energy by not fighting the old, but building the new. Allow that door to close so a new one can be opened.

According to Merriam-Webster *praise* is defined as to glorify (a god or saint) especially by the attribution of perfections. I preached a sermon for a Women's Day program. There was a young lady that performed a liturgical dance that was so compelling and breathe taking. She danced with so much confidence that it shook my soul and brought tears to many. It's amazing how we express ourselves to God and how it captures His heart. In her dance it brought forth deliverance and as Paul and Silas would say everyone's chains were unfastened. So in your praise and worship never hold back, give God all of you and He will give you all of Him.

Let's embrace some moments of some praise and worship that was captured throughout the years. If you have any photos revisit them, do you remember the day or even how you felt in the photo at that very moment? If you don't have any photos, from this day forward capture the moment of your praise so in time of dismay you can encourage yourself.

This is my worship

Journal your thoughts from this chapter:

Chapter 10

My Battle is No Longer a Secret

Self- esteem is defined as confidence in one's own worth or abilities, self-respect. In sociology and psychology self-esteem reflects a person's overall subjective emotional evaluation of his or her worth. First, you must learn to love yourself and sometimes that can be the most challenging thing to do. Although, primarily we struggle in our day to day life, privately not realizing that it shows in our day to day life. Never say anything about yourself that you don't want to come true and never apologize for being you.

Everything in your life is a reflection of the choice you made. If you want a different result make a different choice. Destiny is all about the choices you make and the chances you take. It's not what you are that's holding you back, it's what you think you're not.

List four areas that you feel is holding you back.

_____   _____

_____   _____

Apart of reaching your destiny is understanding your detours. Rise above where you are and start walking into your anointing. You must make a choice to take a chance or your life will never change.

Journal your thoughts from this chapter:

Chapter 11
Transformation Begins

Dear Lord, I ask you to come into my mind. Please begin the process of exposing its images to the light of Your Truth. Help me not to keep albums of negative images that I was never meant to have taken. Help me to place the portrait of Your Son in its place of prominence at the center of the mantle of my mind. Amen

Transformation begins with renewing of the mind. In Romans 12:1-2 it reads, *[1]I beseech you therefore, brethren, by the mercies of God, that ye present your bodies a living sacrifice, holy, acceptable unto God, which is your reasonable service. [2]And be not conformed to this world: but be ye transformed by the renewing of your mind, that ye may prove what is that good, and acceptable, and perfect, will of God. [2]And do not be conformed to this world, but be transformed by the renewing of your mind, so that you may prove what the will of God is, that which is good and acceptable and perfect, will of God.*

What does transformation mean to you? Transformation is defined as 1. The act or process of transforming. 2. the state of being transformed. 3. Change in form, appearance, nature, or character.

Practice the spiritual discipline of meditation by closing your eyes and using your five senses.

What are the five senses? Please list the five senses below:

_____

_____

_____

_____

_____

Mull in your mind that it's God and You. Then pray and ask God to give you insight into the situation and also your life. Ask, what is it about me that I need to deal with? What is it about me that must change?

What about me must I change? Indicate what you must change below:

_____

_____

_____

Now respond to what God is revealing to you by asking him what he wants you to understand. When you understand, respond to God by accepting and admitting whatever responsibility is implied by His revelation. State what it is that God has revealed that you must admit responsibility for doing.
What is that God revealed to you? Indicate what God revealed below:

_____

_____

_____

     Ask God to empower you as an act in obedience, and to accomplish what He has revealed for you to do today.

State below your particular action(s) you will take today to accomplish what God has revealed for you to do.

_____

_____

_____

_____

_____

Give thanks to the Lord
"Thank you, Lord, for what you are doing in me and for what you want me to accomplish in this world through me"

Transformation of the mind is not something which can be accomplished by accident or reached by simply drifting toward it. Jesus disciples are called to choose the life and then live out the life that will renew their minds. It requires a disciplined focus and a change in the way we exercise and train our minds.

In **Philippians 4:6-9 it reads,** *[6]Be careful for nothing; but in everything by prayer and supplication with thanksgiving let your requests be made known unto God. [7]And the peace of God, which passeth all* *understanding, shall keep your hearts and minds through Christ Jesus. ⁸Finally, brethren, whatsoever things are true, whatsoever things are honest, whatsoever things are just, whatsoever things are pure, whatsoever things are lovely, whatsoever things are of good report; if there be any virtue, and if there be any praise, think on these things. ⁹Those things, which ye have both learned, and received, and heard, and seen in me, do: and the God of peace shall be with you.*

This week train your mind to think about change within you. So in life move in the right direction for your life, accept nothing less.

Dear Lord,

Grow me into the kind of spiritual athlete who no longer merely endures these exercises, but has begun to enjoy training my mind. Amen

Journal your thoughts from this chapter:

Chapter 12

Stretch For It

Push forward and put things in the past. The past cannot define, destroy or defeat you. If it's challenging and pushing you, it's helping you become more than you were meant to be. Push forward without hesitation. Say goodbye to yesterday.

Whenever you stretch for something you have to go beyond the norm and captured what it is you're after. I was reading in the Bible where Jesus healed the man whom had a withered hand. In those days you could not do any physical labor, but with the Pharisees didn't understand is that Jesus when He healed the man he did not break any laws. In fact all that really mattered to them was their narrow interpretation of things.

I realize when you're going into the next level in life you can't worry about who isn't going with you, sometimes it may require you to go by yourself. Jesus could've healed the man in a private environment, but instead he called the man out into the crowd so everyone could see His works and when you're going in the next level in God everyone will be able to see what God is doing. So we have to give God praise for our today and all of your yesterdays that took you through hell.

List four areas that you have to stretch beyond and how do you plan on doing.

1. _____
2. _____
3. _____
4. _____

Life is too short and everything happens for a reason. So don't be discourage just continue to stretch for it. If you get a chance- take it; if it changes your life- let it. Beloved never stop fighting until you are at the place in your life that you are predestined to be. Everything you have you owe God, so stretch for it.

Journal your thoughts from this chapter:

Chapter 13

On the Wrong Road at the Wrong Time

Sometimes people whether old or young are so determined to go down the wrong road. It is as if their minds were taken over by whatever desire they're fixated on. The Bible made reference that a certain man went to Jerusalem to Jericho. Jericho was a placed filled with wickedness and it was so pervasive that immortality degradation, and barbarity invaded every facet of life. Children were sacrificed to pagan gods; there was male and female prostitution that took place right inside of the temple which were a part of religious riots. This evil was so contagious that God's people were endangered as well. All of this took place on the road Jericho, a seventeen mile road that connects from Jerusalem to Jericho. The road drops three thousand six hundred feet. It is a steep, winding, descending and remote road that for centuries has been a place where thieves and robbers congregate.

The Bible tells us that David took a trip down to Jericho road but even David had sense enough not to go down this road by himself. David took the Lord with him. Psalms 23: 4-5 Yea, though I walk through the valley of the shadow of death, I will fear no evil; For You *are* with me; Your rod and Your staff, they comfort me. ⁵ You prepare a table before me in the presence of my enemies; you anoint my head with oil; my cup runs over. David was talking about the Jericho road, I realized once you start to fall in your life you start to go down. Whenever you leave God's covenant and grace you go down. As a Christian when began resent church and discontinue your fellowship you also go down slowly, in other words you get spiritually disconnect and wonder into the wrong direction. I noticed that the enemy doesn't bother you when you up and praising God, he waits until you starts to fall at the most vulnerable time in your life. The enemy rather you be down in your spirit, thinking and decision making. So allow God to order your steps concerning your life.

List four areas you need directions in:

_____

_____

_____

_____

Rewinding time is not possible, but a do-over is. Sometimes we get another chance to do something right the second time that we got wrong the first time. Life is too short. Time is too fast. There is no reply or rewind, so make every day count.

Journal your thoughts from this chapter:

Chapter 14
I Found a Way Out

Some people are standing in the middle of their pain, disappointment, and struggle. In applying the word of God in your life, it will help you unlock the door to what you need in order to move in the right direction. Often, the enemy keeps us busy because he doesn't want us to deal with our baggage. I'm sure we all can attest to the fact that we have been hurt at some point in our lives by someone. There are some people that don't understand their worth, value or purpose and we get frustrated, losing our sense of direction. We get so close to our exit resulting in consumption of our emotions that we turn away from where we need to be. In some many occasions God has pulled us out of a complex situation only to find that we want to go back to it.

Proverbs reads you're like a dog returning back to your vomit. I want to cautious those of you that are in ministry, leadership or working in your purpose to never to a place where you allow your emotions to push you out of your position. In addition, never get to a place where you allow people less than you to get the best of you. I want to serve notice and inform you that I found a way out. I need an emergency exit, I've found a way out of hurt, abuse, taken for granted, underestimated and rejected. I'm getting ready to slide right on out.

In life move in the right direction for your life, accept nothing less; allow God to help you make a way out.

Journal your thoughts from this chapter:

Chapter 15

Write it all down to get it all out….

In this chapter, journal what you feel on a day to day basis, review what you've written and respond to it. To get you started below are some of my past weekly thoughts, please review and respond with your thoughts. The following activity you will then try on your own.

Monday: What the mind holds. You'll never know how long your words will stay in someone's mind even long after you've forgotten you spoke them. Words are seeds they do more than blow around. They land in our hearts, not on the ground. Be careful of what you plant and be careful of what you say, because you might have to eat what you plant one day. Always watch what you say.

_____
_____
_____
_____
_____

Tuesday: Be mindful sometimes you will never know the true value of a moment until it becomes a memory. In my own experience I have learned that everything has value even if you put it on the shelf and let it collect dust. Someone is going to come along, take it off the shelf, wipe the dust off, shine it up and see the value.

_____
_____
_____
_____

Wednesday: Marathon time--You can run all you want, but the baggage that you travel with will continue to hold you down until you let some of it go. It's time to unpack and walk away from your baggage.

_____
_____
_____
_____

Thursday: As you breathe in think because as you take another breath someone else takes their last. Please don't complain about something you do not have control of, just appreciate life.

_____
_____
_____
_____

Friday: The deeper the scar the greater the VICTORY; The woman in me.

_____
_____
_____
_____

Saturday: Stop staying with someone who hurts and does not appreciate you. It is not romantic or beautiful. What's beautiful is moving on. Focusing on yourself and loving who you are. Introduce yourself to people you are flower getting ready to bloom.

_____
_____
_____
_____
_____

Sunday: A person's character is shown through their actions in life, not where they sit on Sunday morning. The question is do you know we're your sitting?

_____
_____
_____
_____
_____

Now it's your turn to journal, review and respond to your thoughts.

Monday:_____

_____

_____

_____

_____

Tuesday:_____

_____

_____

_____

_____

Wednesday:_____

_____

_____

_____

_____

Thursday:_____

_____

_____

Friday:_____

Saturday:_____

Sunday:_____

Journal your thoughts from this chapter:

Chapter 16
Dare to Believe

What is the difference between those who have experienced their breakthroughs and those who are still trapped by toxic emotions and their habit forming addictions? The answer is simple, it how we believe. If you believe you will succeed you will, if you believe that you won't you won't. As a man or woman thinks so is he/she, our perception of ourselves plays a major role on our overall outcome and no one can control what you think but you.

I'm a believer but if you can change what you believe, you can change your life. Learn to see what God sees and win the battle over your mind. When I'm worried, it's usually because I'm trying to do everything myself and when I am at peace it usually because God is in control. Sometimes it's best to stay out of your own way. I realize the battle people face from day to day are real and when we face life in its truth we can face anything. We first have to accept accountability, be accountable for what you have done by first forgiving yourself and then ask others to forgive you and/or you forgive others. I think one of the hardest things for a person to do is to forgive themselves. I often ponder in my mind about the mercies of God and how He forgave us for all of our sins. Also how He gave His only begotten Son as a sacrifice for us. John 8:32 The Bible reads, *and you shall know the truth, and truth shall make you free.* This is a verse that has been widely used.

What does it really means to you?

_____

_____

_____

_____

What is the truth that sets you free?

_____

_____

_____

Everything in your life is a reflection of the choices you have made. If you want a different result concerning your life, then make a different choice and dare to believe that the choices you made will positively impact your life, allowing you to access your God giving purpose, "dare to believe".

Dear You,
Make peace with the mirror and watch your reflection change. The secret of change is to focus all of your energy on what you believe. Love you.

Journal your thoughts from this chapter:

Chapter 17
Leave it Up to Him

Trust God, Obey God and leave the consequence up to God. A woman or man of God does not negotiate the call on his or her life, focus on the vision in front of you.

Greater is He that is in you. The only person that you are destined to become is the person you are destined to be. When you are destined for greatness everything around you changes. Sometimes you have to take a step back and acknowledge what's important in your life. What you can live with , but most importantly what you can't live without. So, don't let something that's long gone continue to control you, it's time to let go. Sometimes, you need to step outside, get some air and remind yourself who you are and who you want to be. Beloved keep pushing forward.

As we go through life everything you do is based on the choices you make. It is not your parents, husband, wife, job, past relationships, economy, an argument nor age that is to blame. However, you must learn to trust

God and leave up to Him to restore, repair and place the things concerning you.

What do you need to leave up to Him to handle?

1. _____
2. _____
3. _____
4. _____
5. _____
6. _____
7. _____
8. _____
9. _____
10. _____

Journal your thoughts from this chapter:

Chapter 18
There is a Place for You

In Acts 28:1-6 it reads, [1] *When we were safely ashore, we learned that the island was called Malita.* [2] *The natives there were very friendly to us. It had started to rain and was cold, so they built a fire and made us all welcome.* [3] *Paul gathered up a bundle of sticks and was putting them on the fire when a snake came out on account of the heat and fastened itself to his hand.* [4] *The natives saw the snake hanging on Paul's hand and said to one another, this man must be a murderer, but fate will not let him live, even though he escaped from the sea.* [5] *But Paul shook the snake off into the fire without being harmed at all.* [6] *They were waiting for him to swell up or suddenly fall down dead. But after waiting for a long time and not seeing anything unusual happening to him, they changed their minds and said he is a god!*

Our text deals with a tremendous Bible character. Saul of Tarsus was no peon, but he was a man of greatness, and his presence in the New Testament church brought great wealth and growth. He established ministries, he wrote much of the new testaments and the Epistles. He was somebody that God favored and chose to use but somehow being used by God was synonymous of being tried.

God for some reason doesn't give greatness to people that hasn't being proven yet. He doesn't anoint you if you don't know how to handle being anointed. He won't give you revelation, if you are going to be self-center and arrogant. You can spend all of your nights in your commentaries if you please, but if you don't know how to humbly submit yourself under the mighty hand of God, then he cannot and will not give you divined authority.

Most of us know that many are the afflictions of the righteous and the Lord delivers us out of them. I trust him enough to praise him in advance, even before I go in it I know I'm coming out of it. ***Hallelujah!***

When Abraham took Isaac to the mountain top to use him as a sacrifice, he indicated to those that accompanied him to wait that he and Isaac would be returning. How in the world do you come down again with a boy that God has asked you to use as a sacrifice? When things gets bad just declare and call forth those things that are not as though they were. Things may look like it's going to be terrible but speak peace. Even if it looks like it's going to be disastrous I know that God is going to make a way.

In life don't let conditions intimidate you and don't let the night times of your life cause you to be bullied and retreat. But tell the night that comes to try you that you are only here for a season, because God has so arranged it in the chronological order of time that after every night there is going to be a morning. And I heard the Bible say weeping may endure for a night, but joy comes in the morning.

Malita represents a place allegorically and metaphorically of where we are tried after just being tried. It is the place that before I can regroup, catch my breath and get myself together I'm being attacked again. However, it's alright because I know I'm going somewhere.

Also know that Malita is the last stop before Paul got to Rome. Rome is the place where Paul had been ordained to go. A place where he was going to stand before the Sanhedrims; A place where he was going to preach to the astrologers, philosophers and preached to those who didn't believe that Jesus was the Messiah. When you exercise your faith through the power of God you can shake off the snake bites of my enemies, jealous people and haters.

List four things in your life you need to shake off
1. _____
2. _____
3. _____
4. _____

Journal your thoughts from this chapter:

Chapter 19

At the Point of No Return

In Isaiah 43:18-19 NKJ [18] Remember ye not the former things, neither consider the things of old. [19] Behold, I will do a new thing; now it shall spring forth; shall ye not know it? I will even make a way in the wilderness, and rivers in the desert.

When reading the text in verse 18, before we can appreciate this blessing in this particular passage we have to first understand the process. The word process means a series of actions, changes or steps to achieve an expected end. So in order for you to go into a new season we have to go through this process. Refer back to verse 18; God is trying to condition our minds to forget every and anything that would cause us not to move forward. I want to share a few scenarios with you.

1. Have you ever been in a relationship where you are trying to move forward and find yourself competing with the person you are with?

2. Have you been in a relationship that's simply out of convenience and nothing about it says "yes"?

   In order to achieve this process you have to believe in your mind and heart. In Romans 12:2 reads, [2] And be not conformed to this world: but be ye transformed by the renewing of your mind, that ye may prove what is that good, and acceptable, and perfect, will of God.

The process is having a renewed mind, changing your way of thinking will renew your life. You have to say to self, "that I am at the point of no return". In order to break the chain of a toxic relationship you have to be at the point of no return. Also in order to break the chain of alcohol and or drugs you have to be at the point of no return.

In order to break the chain of imprisonment and unfaithfulness you have to be desperate and at the point of no return. How many of you are desperate? Are you desperate for your break through? Are you desperate to be free from spiritual bondage? Let us say this prayer,

Dear Father,

I am standing in the need of prayer, healing and restoration. I am desperate for you and change. Even in my struggles I still look to you to redeem me and hide me. Although I stumble you never let me fall when I'm weak you give me strength, creating me a clean heart and give me the right attitude to approach every situation in my life with gratitude and thanks. Thank you for being the keeper of my thoughts even when I want to turn away, you know how to draw me closer to you. Lord I'm desperate for you, thank you for setting me free and for total restoration. I am free no longer am I bound, I am set free. Selah

Journal your thoughts from this chapter:

Chapter 20

God's Promise to You is Behind the Wall

In the Book of Joshua 6: 1-7 it reads. Now the gates of Jericho were tightly shut because the people were afraid of the Israelites. No one was allowed to go out or in. [2] But the LORD said to Joshua, "I have given you Jericho, its king, and all its strong warriors. [3] You and your fighting men should march around the town once a day for six days. [4] Seven priests will walk ahead of the Ark, each carrying a ram's horn. On the seventh day you are to march around the town seven times, with the priests blowing the horns. [5] When you hear the priests give one long blast on the rams' horns, have all the people shout as loud as they can. Then the walls of the town will collapse, and the people can charge straight into the town." [6] So Joshua called together the priests and said, "Take up the Ark of the LORD's Covenant, and assign seven priests to walk in front of it, each carrying a ram's horn." [7] Then he gave orders to the people: "March around the town, and the armed men will lead the way in front of the Ark of the LORD."

    I want to impart some wisdom into your lives on today concerning on how God can and will reward you for following His instructions on how to live according to His will. Some of you on today are having a hard time trying to figure out why God hasn't come to your rescue. It's not because he doesn't know your struggles, employment conditions, or even your day to day situation, believe me God sees all and knows all. Just remember He is that same God that knows every hair that is on your head. So God understands your situation, but are you willing to turn away from your sinful ways and give our God your best efforts and follow Him?

    Like in Israel the people finally crossed the Jordan. They prepared themselves spiritually and up to that point had followed God's orders to the letter. Now, they are ready to begin the conquest of the Promised Land. They are ready to claim for themselves the land that flowed with milk and honey.

Now, just for a moment, try to put yourself into the shoes of the average Israelite soldier. For most of these men, Jericho was the first city they had ever seen that was surrounded by huge walls. It must have looked like an absolute impossible task. However, they listened to the instructions they were given by the Lord and they saw those massive walls fall down flat.

You may be wondering why we are studying events that took place so long ago and so far away. What does all of this have to do with our lives? How does all of this apply to my life as a believer? We as a people know we are living in days of battle and spiritual struggle. We need to know how to fight and how to claim our dreams and prosperity that God has for us. We need to know that our God has given us the victory and we should follow Him to which was given.

Our study of Joshua teaches us those valuable lessons! Just as Israel faced the mighty walls of Jericho, you and I face walls and obstacles in our lives as well. We need to know how to overcome them as we march towards the victory and promises that God has for us.

List four obstacles (walls) in your life you want to fall down:

_____

_____

_____

_____

When life is filled with adversities, know that you can walk in victory and purpose. Don't allow the enemy to down play who you are in God, get up bout face and let's move forward and watch all your walls fall.

Now that your walls have fallen, what was your process to gain the results? Be sure to apply the process in your daily lives so that it will never be repeated.

_____

_____

_____

_____

_____

Journal your thoughts from this chapter:

Chapter 21
Rebound to Build

Psalm 30: 1-5 reads 1 I will extol thee, O Lord; for thou hast lifted me up, and hast not made my foes to rejoice over me. 2 O Lord my God, I cried unto thee, and thou hast healed me. 3 O Lord, thou hast brought up my soul from the grave: thou hast kept me alive, that I should not go down to the pit. 4 Sing unto the Lord, O ye saints of his, and give thanks at the remembrance of his holiness. 5 For his anger endureth but a moment; in his favor is life: weeping may endure for a night, but joy cometh in the morning.

Saints life is always a kaleidoscope of conflicting experiences and emotions and we find this very variety reflected in the contents of this 30th Psalm, by the way not all psalms are the same. Some of them are majestic hymns of praise to God, reflecting the joy of the jubilant worshipper who is at peace with God and with the world. By contrast, others reflect the darker moments of human experience; feelings of guilt feature in some of them, while others consist of songs of protection, complaining about unjust suffering.

Let's journey back to this ancient time to visit and talk to David, let's find out what he was thinking about when he wrote this particular Psalm at that moment of time. I want to know what were you going through and why God heard your cry after what you've done.

What is forgiveness, it is defined as to excuse for a fault or an offense, to pardon; to renounce anger or resentment against. Forgiveness runs deep, it is not a thin surface patched on a relationship, but rather an inner change of heart towards the offender. Too often we think we have extended forgiveness when in reality we have only covered over our resentment.

The Greek word for forgiveness is Nasa, similar to the word exhale, which means to get it out of you. You don't want it to choke you or stop your flow of breathing. What takes a toll on your heart is when one doesn't forgive; when you cover up resentment, faults, and excuses. When you don't renounce your anger at someone or when you don't pardon them in your hearts of hearts, what takes place in your heart is a buildup of stress, guilt, and frustration. Also when we don't forgive it takes a toll in our bodies, it takes an effect on our physical well-being and may simply result in deterioration. It is when you release people that you have not forgiven or their forgiveness for you has not transpired. Some of you haven't forgiven yourselves and when you don't release this toxic waste, "if you will" it opens up medical and emotional consequences, but whenever you do you can have peace, joy, and a pure heart. Amen.

Forgiveness can release super natural breakthroughs in your life. But it starts with the word forgive. As a Christian we know that you may get your feelings hurt, be angry, and be disappointed by others, but you have to learn how to get over it and forgive one another. You have to receive and give forgiveness. If you are going to do great things as a Christian, then you are going to have great offenses. Amen

God will promote those who can take offenses. And he will equip you so that you can defeat this enemy of harboring this toxic waste in order for you to continue the job he has design for you in the Kingdom of God. You can't be promoted people of God if you can't take offenses. Your ability to shake things off and see the bigger picture will determine how successful you will be in this walk with Jesus Christ. Don't give the enemy the power over you but instead understand that this toxic waste can prevent you from your breakthroughs, blessings, and even your promotions in the Kingdom of God.

So whoever you need to forgive please do, whether it's a wife, husband, ex-wife, or ex-husband, child, brother, sister, mother, father, relative, or friend, please don't allow this to cause you to choke, just forgive them. I forgive you.

Why is it important for you to forgive?

_____

_____

_____

_____

Journal your thoughts from this chapter:

Chapter 22

I'm Not Running Back to You

After you have been damaged in a relationship and or marriage and trust is involved. First, you must work on building trust again. Building trust back into a relationship that has been damaged by sexual integrity issues is like building with Lego's. Some of the pieces include time, energy, planning, vision, patience, hope and commitment.

Trust building is an ongoing process that constitutes multiple factors that with time you piece together. However in reality there is not set formula to rebuild trust. The process cannot be prescribed by any doctor or calculated by any mathematician. I've learned through the course of life if you love God first then you can love anyone else. One of the biggest problems that I have witnessed in relationships or marriages are the words "I give up". We give up when we don't feel we are worthy of our relationship or marriage. People must realize if you don't feel worthy it will show in every aspect of your life, understand that people will give you only what you feel you deserve.

In any relationship or marriage it is a simple solution, be careful of the words you choose and how you choose them because the words you speak show people who you really are. Once you have said something you cannot take it back, so practice what you say in a relationship or marriage before you say it. When trust is broken sometimes it makes it difficult for people to get past or go beyond what has happened to them, however the beautiful thing is that God tells us if we have a mountain in our lives all we have to do is say to the mountain or speak to it, trust God and it shall be removed. The key is the exercising of your faith; faith simplifies the things that we hope for and gives us evidence of things that are not seen. What is not seen is realizing that we can do all things through Christ who gives us strength. God gives us the strength to rebound, overcome, and face whatever situation that is thrown at us. I would like to leave you with a thought, trust will be restored when you decide to forgive and that is my prayer.

Do you have issues with trust? List four areas in your relationship or marriage you would like to overcome?

_____

_____

_____

_____

Journal your thoughts from this chapter:

Chapter 23
Purpose to Succeed

Purpose is the reason which something is done or created, a person's sense of determination. Succeed is to achieve your desired aim or result. As I was pondering what the Iphone Siri defined what the meaning of purpose and succeed were, it made me embrace the moment and I saw it this way:

Success to me is like your own shadow, if you try to catch it you will never succeed, ignore it walk in your own way and it will follow you; when the world says "Give up", hope whispers and says "try one more time". Now I want you to gather in your mindset on your purpose to succeed and write it down:

_____

_____

_____

_____

As I shared my insight to help readers adjust to many changes that life brings. In reading this book I hope it will shake you up and that mind will be transformed. We should all be willing to make adjustments that are necessary to our lives and should also be able to see and identify with ourselves so that we can meet, face and deal with who we really are. Let every page in this book inspire you to rise above where you are and start walking into your divine purpose. This is my prayer for you.

Father,

As a believer I challenge myself to first love me, love who I am and how you made me. I realize that my struggles are real and I know that I will overcome every adversity that I am face with. Thank you for giving me insight and direction, for in that how can we learn unless we've been taught, I accept responsibility and accountability. I am more than a conqueror and I will no longer live in lack but I will work in prosperity. I will no longer be discouraged nor defeated. For I know that I am fearfully and wonderfully made by you. And I accept who I am and I see who I am. In Jesus' name Amen.

Journal your thoughts from this chapter:

Scripture References

The Holy Bible King James Version Large Print Thinline Reference edition, Hendrickson Publisher. MA, Second Printing Hendrickson Publisher Edition. November 2010

Joshua 6: 1-7

Psalms 30: 1-5

Romans 12: 2

I Corinthians 7: 28

I Corinthians 7: 32-34

Matthew 19: 11

I Corinthians 7: 7

Romans 12:1-2

Ecclesiastes 4:12

Genesis 1: 27-28

Mark 10: 9

Acts 28:1-6

Ecclesiastes 9:9

I Peter 4:8

Ephesians 4:2-3

Hebrew 13:4

Philippians 4:6-9

Acts 16: 25-26

Isaiah 43: 18-19

John 8:32

Merriam Webster, https://www.merriam-webster.com/ 2017 Merriam-Webster, Incorporated

Iphone Siri, 2017 Apple Incorporated

Made in the USA
Columbia, SC
03 September 2022